ISBN: 978-1-85103-443-7

Originally published as *Ella Fitzgerald* by Editions Gallimard Jeunesse

© & ℗ 2011 Editions Gallimard Jeunesse

This edition was published in the United Kingdom by Moonlight Publishing Ltd,

36 Innovation Drive, Milton Park, Abingdon, Oxon, OX14 4RT

English text © & ℗ 2016 Moonlight Publishing Ltd

Printed in China

ELLA
Fitzgerald

FIRST DISCOVERY MUSIC

Illustrated by Rémi Courgeon
Written by Stéphane Ollivier
Narrated by John Chancer

Born in Newport News, Virginia, on the East Coast of the United States, on April 25, 1917, Ella Fitzgerald is only a toddler when her parents separate. Her young mother, Tempie, decides to move to the

A TOUCH OF THE BLUES

The blues came into being in the 20th century in the cotton fields of the United States. The haunting melodies of songs sung by African-American slaves carry all the pent-up feeling and misery of their condition. They were to have a great influence on jazz. Do you ever sing to yourself when you are sad?

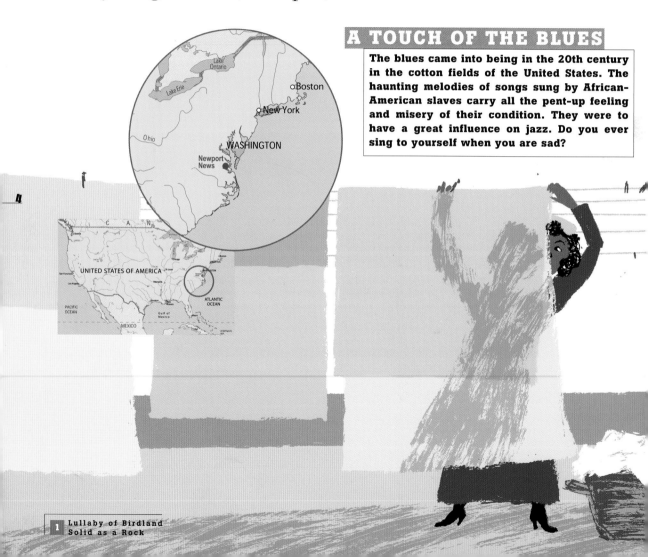

4

1 Lullaby of Birdland
Solid as a Rock

suburbs of New York where her sister lives. Tempie finds work in a laundry. She also meets a new partner, Joseph Da Silva. A few years later, Ella's half-sister, Frances, is born. Things are looking up.

Ella grows up in a poor neighbourhood where people from many different cultural backgrounds, including African Americans and immigrants from Italy and Eastern Europe, rub shoulders happily, speaking different languages. Ella is a high-spirited, happy-go-lucky child, and a real tomboy, who loves

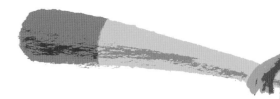

BEYOND BORDERS

A song sung in another language doesn't necessarily sound strange. Music is in itself a language we all share and which moves us in different ways. Are there any songs, in French or Spanish maybe, that you like to sing, even if you can't speak the language itself?

The United States became a real haven for immigrants from all over the world. Between 1892 and 1924, 16 million sailed to New York.

joining in games of baseball in the neighbourhood. But life is not easy. Money is short and Ella has to run errands after school to earn a dollar or two to help make ends meet.

The first official game of baseball was played in 1846. It evolved from older bat and ball games. Long the national sport, it is still one of the most popular in the USA.

Ella develops a real taste for the music she listens to day and night on the family radio. She likes Duke Ellington with his big orchestra and Mamie Smith singing blues, but she prefers romantic songs sung by female variety singers like the Boswell Sisters. As she has

3 Was that the Human Thing to do?
Mack the Knife (by Louis Armstrong and then by Ella Fitzgerald)

a good ear and a strong sense of rhythm, she soon becomes the star of the school choir. Her imitations of Louis Armstrong's powerful, rasping voice are much appreciated by her classmates.

OVER TO YOU!

Did you know that seven different notes are all you need to play music? Do re, mi, fa, so, la, ti... and that's it! Once you learn these notes you can play any piece you like, even take up a small instrument. Practise a tune you like and get your family to come and listen.

Although the first radios were invented at the end of the 19th century, music transmissions were not broadcast until the 1920s.

Mamie Smith was a great blues singer of the 1920s. She was also a dancer, actress and pianist.

At thirteen, Ella is small for her age, and unhappy about the way she looks. She is lacking in self-confidence. But when she tries out the latest popular dance routines, she moves so well to the beat that her dancing attracts attention. She becomes quite a

local celebrity by imitating the crazy, undulating hip movements of Earl 'Snakehips' Tucker. She dreams of being able to perform at the Savoy Ballroom, the great concert hall in Harlem. What is to stop her becoming a dancer?

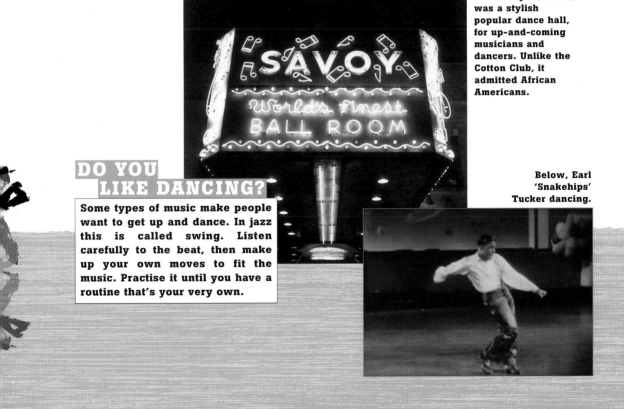

The Savoy Ballroom, was a stylish popular dance hall, for up-and-coming musicians and dancers. Unlike the Cotton Club, it admitted African Americans.

Below, Earl 'Snakehips' Tucker dancing.

DO YOU LIKE DANCING?

Some types of music make people want to get up and dance. In jazz this is called swing. Listen carefully to the beat, then make up your own moves to fit the music. Practise it until you have a routine that's your very own.

Egged on by her friends, Ella decides to take part in an amateur dance and singing competition organised by the Apollo Theatre in Harlem. She is only 17 and is intimidated by an impressive local dance duo that go before her. When it is her turn to get up and dance on stage, she is paralysed with fear and cannot move. To save face she

12

STAGE FRIGHT

People who perform in front of an audience (singers, musicians, actors) sometimes get what we call stage fright. It can make them feel very nervous, but it can also help them perform even better than they might have done. Maybe this has happened to you when you had to get up in class and recite a poem?

It was the Boswell Sisters' song *Object of my Affection* that Ella chose to sing as an encore when she won that first competition.

suddenly decides to sing instead. At first the audience boos, but soon they fall silent, captivated by the clear voice of the young girl, who gradually gains confidence as she sings. By the end of her first song they are calling for an encore. Ella wins the competition, not as a dancer but as a singer!

Everybody agrees: the tone of her voice is pure, her range excellent. She has exceptional talent. But a jazz singer needs to be attractive and no band leader will look twice at a rather shy, awkward young girl like her. When Tempie dies suddenly of a heart attack, Ella is

broken-hearted. What will become of her now? Lonely, unemployed, and homeless at times, she wanders the streets of Harlem. Putting on a brave smile, she goes back to doing the rounds of the clubs. But her future is looking bleak!

FINDING HER VOICE

The human voice is a remarkable instrument. Each and every one is different: deep, gravelly, velvety, reedy, high-pitched, shrill... To sing well, you need to know how to use your voice and pitch it. Have you ever sung in a choir?

One evening Ella is approached by an unusual character, Chick Webb. He is hunchbacked and only 4 feet (1 m 20) tall. But he is an outstanding drummer and his band is one of the best in Harlem. Webb is touched by Ella's openness and above all he recognises in her someone of outstanding talent. He offers her a contract. When her rendering of *A-Tisket, A-Tasket* reaches Number 1 in the hit parade, there is no doubt about it, her career is launched!

16

Chick Webb on drums, with a smiling Ella.

7 A-Tisket, A-Tasket

Today

as in the past...

we listen to

and enjoy

the music of

Ella

FITZGERALD

HOW HIGH THE MOON?

The great fluidity and range of Ella Fitzgerald's voice and her extraordinarily precise sense of rhythm make her a remarkable improviser. She is attracted to a new complex form of jazz called bebop. Here she is giving a spirited and very modern rendering of the song *How High the Moon*. Notice how she replaces words with a series of invented, expressive sounds. Ella's voice becomes a musical instrument which she plays with great skill. This way of singing, which is typical of jazz, is known as 'scat'. Ella stands out as a past master of this art.

18

The craze for 'swing' (very lively music which makes you want to dance) grew up in the 1930s in the African-American quarters of large towns. Clarinettist and band leader, Benny Goodman, nicknamed the 'King of Swing' (seen below), is responsible for making swing popular all over the United States.

In the search for more freedom, individual musicians from the great jazz bands form smaller groups, improvising and performing solo: the result is an entirely new style of jazz, bebop, with Charlie Parker (left) and Dizzy Gillespie (right).

BEWITCHED...

In the 1950s, Ella undertakes a very personal reading and reinterpretation of the whole repertoire of American songwriting. The popular songs written between 1920 and 1940 for Broadway musicals were composed by musicians like George Gershwin and Cole Porter. In her rendering of Richard Rodgers' *Bewitched, Bothered and Bewildered,* Ella remains faithful to the melody, and plays instead on the meaning of the words, as an actress might. The way she weaves her voice into the rhythm and combines it with the swing of the pianist's counterpoint make it a remarkable example of jazz at its purest.

20

During the 1930s and 40s, Cole Porter wrote the songs and composed the music for some of the most famous American musicals of all time.

ella fitzgerald sings the cole porter song book

The 1920s was a golden age for Broadway musicals combining dance, singing, humour and catchy music in very colourful performances.

Times Square on Broadway was one of the highlights of the vibrant, brightly-lit theatre district of New York, home to over 40 theatres.

9 Bewitched, Bothered and Bewildered, 1956

JINGLE BELLS

In the course of the 1960s Ella enjoys more and more recognition outside the jazz circle. The 'First Lady of Song', as she is now known, sings increasingly with variety bands. She sings every style of music, and becomes one of the most popular performers in the United States, ranking with stars such as Frank Sinatra. The recording she makes of *Jingle Bells* in 1960, and dedicates to Christmas, stands in the great tradition of American music hall. It is a masterpiece of humour and vocal skill, but also a perfect example of swing!

22

Frank Sinatra was one of the most famous 20th century singers of popular music. He was known as *The Voice* because of the rich, velvety timbre of his singing voice.

Jingle Bells, the popular Christmas song you probably know by heart, was composed by the American, James Lord Pierpoint, in 1957.

IT DON'T MEAN A THING

Throughout her career, it is on stage, and surrounded by great jazz musicians like Duke Ellington, the composer, pianist and bandleader of a jazz orchestra you see opposite, that Ella Fitzgerald gives her very best. This exuberant and original version of one of Duke's great standards, where Ella talks and jokes with the band's musicians, brings to mind the playful, friendly banter of the improvisation, or 'jam sessions' as they are known, which are typical of jazz. The mixture of humour and swing is the very essence of the festive spirit this music expresses.

24

Jam sessions gave musicians a chance to be even more creative. Left, Duke Ellington jamming. Opposite, Ella with Duke.

Ella with another jazz giant, Louis Armstrong.

MOONLIGHT PUBLISHING

Translator:
Penelope Stanley-Baker

English narration recording:
John Chancer

GALLIMARD JEUNESSE

Gallimard Jeunesse Musique:
Paule du Bouchet

Artistic direction:
Élisabeth Cohat

Design:
Yann Le Duc

Layout:
Anne-Catherine Boudet

LIST OF ILLUSTRATIONS

4l Map of the USA, © Géoatlas, Graphi-Ogre, 2000. **6** Immigrants on the bridge of a boat passing in front of the Statue of Liberty in the Port of New York in 1887, engraving. © The Granger Collection NYC / Rue des Archives. **7** Street scene in 1920, boys playing baseball, © Getty images – Photo by Lewis W. Hine, collection: George Eastman House. **9t** Radio tube vintage, © Tony Ramos Photography / Shutterstock. **9b** Mamie Smith (1883-1946), Joseph Samuel's Jazz Band, 1921, Willie 'The Lion' on piano, Gavin Bushell, Herb Flemming, Everett Robbins, Julius Berkin, Joseph Samuels, © Rue des Archives / BCA. **11t** The neon lights of the Savoy Dance Club, Harlem, New York City, 1947 © Getty Images / Hulton Archive. **11b** Earl 'Snakehips' Tucker dancing, © D. R. **12** Signed photograph of the Boswell Sisters, about 1935, © Getty Images / Michael Ochs Archives. **16l** Photograph of Chick Webb on drums, around 1935, © Getty Images / Michael Ochs Archives. **16r** Ella Fitzgerald, 1940, © Library of Congress / Carl Van Vechten / D. R. **18t** Benny Goodman's Band, in the 1940s, © Rue des Archives / BCA. **18b** Saxophonist and Black American Jazz, Charlie Parker (1920-1955) with Dizzy Gillespy (1917-1993) in March 1951, © Rue des Archives / AGIP. **19** Ella Fitzgerald (1917-1996) American jazz singer, with Bill Beason on drums, Dick Vance and Irving Randolph playing trumpet in the Savoy Ballroom, New York, 1941, © Rue des Archives / AGIP. **20t** Cole Porter (1893-1964), American composer, working at the piano, © Rue des Archives / BCA. **20t** Sleeve of the record *Ella Fitzgerald sings the Cole Porter Songbook*, Verve / Universal Music. **20b** Ray Bolger (1904-1987), American actor playing in the Broadway Review 'Three to Make Ready', 1946. © Getty Images FPG / Hulton Archive. **20m** Dancers in the show 'Fancy Free' by Jerome Robbins, dancing on the streets of Broadway in 1958, © Time & Life Pictures / Getty Images. **20b** View of Times Square, 1940, © Getty Images. **21** Ella Fitzgerald, 1960, © Rue des Archives / FIA. **22** Frank Sinatra and Ella Fitzgerald side by side in 1950, © Rue des Archives / AGIP. **22m** Sleeves of records *Frank Sinatra sings Great American Songbook*, © Acrobat ACMCD4268 and *Ella wishes You a Swinging Christmas*, © Verve/Universal Music. **22b** Christmas decorations in the Rockefeller Plaza, New York in the 1950's. **23** Ella Fitzgerald, around 1950, © Rue des Archives / BCA. **24** Poster for a concert with Duke Ellington and his Cotton Club band, 1930s. © The Granger Collection NYC / Rue des Archives. **24m** Duke Ellington playing *Sophisticated Lady* at a jam session. **24b** Ella Fitzgerald and Louis Armstrong, 1956, © UA / Rue des Archives. **25** Ella Fitzgerald and Duke Ellington at the piano, around 1970. © Bettmann / CORBIS.

KEY: **t**=top   **m**=middle   **b**=bottom
      r=right   **l**=left

1 **Lullaby of Birdland**
George Shearing – George Weiss)
Ella Fitzgerald: vocals
Raymond Tunia: piano
Ray Brown: double bass
Buddy Rich: drums
Recorded on September 17, 1954
at Jazz at the Philharmonic, Hartford,
Connecticut.

Solid as a Rock
Bob Hilliard – David Mann)
Sy Oliver and his band
Ella Fitzgerald: vocals
Bernie Privin, Tony Faso,
Paul Webster: trumpet
Handerson Chambers: trombone
Milt Yaner, Did Cooper: alto saxophone
Jerry Jerome, Al Klink: tenor saxophone
Hank Jones: piano
Everett Barksdale: guitar
Ray Brown: double bass
Jimmy Crawford: drums
Recorded in New York on March 6, 1950.

2 **Swingin' Shepherd Blues**
Moe Koffman – Kenny Jacobson –
Rhoda Roberts)
Ella Fitzgerald: vocals
Harry 'Sweets' Edison: trumpet
Other unnamed musicians
Recorded in Los Angeles on March 19, 1958.

3 **Was that the Human Thing to do?**
Sammy Fain – Joe Young)
Boswell Sisters: vocals
Dorsey Brothers band
Bunny Berigan: trumpet
Tommy Dorsey: trombone
Jimmy Dorsey: clarinet, alto saxophone
Joe Venuti: violin
Arthur Schutt: piano
Eddie Lang: guitar
Recorded on February 5, 1932.

Mack the Knife
Kurt Weill – Bertolt Brecht – Marc Blitzstein)
Ella Fitzgerald: vocals
Paul Smith: piano
Jim Hall: guitar
Wilfred Middlebrooks: double bass
Gus Johnson: drums
Recorded in Deutschlandhalleoon, West Berlin
on February 13, 1960.

• Louis Armstrong and the All Stars
Louis Armstrong: trumpet, vocals
James Osborne 'Trummy' Young: trombone
Edmond Hall: clarinet
William Osborne ('Billy Kyle'): piano
Arwell Shaw: double bass
Barrett Deems: drums
Recorded in Carnegie Hall, New York
on March 17, 1956.

4 **Rockin'in Rhythm**
Duke Ellington and His Orchestra:
Cat Anderson, Willie Cook, Ray Nance
or Harold 'Shorty' Baker
Clark Terry: trumpet
Quentin Jackson, Britt Woodman,
John Sanders: trombone
Jimmy Hamilton: clarinet, tenor saxophone
Russell Procope: alto saxophone, clarinet
Johnny Hodges: alto saxophone
Frank Foster: tenor saxophone
Harry Carney: bassoon, bass clarinet,
clarinet
Duke Ellington: piano
Jimmy Woode: double bass
Sam Woodyard: drums

5 **Get Happy**
(Harold Arlen – Ted Koehler)
Ella Fitzgerald: vocals
Billy May and his band
Ted Nash: alto saxophone
Paul Smith: piano
John Collins , Al Hendrickson: guitar
Joe Mondragon: double bass
Alvin Stoller: drums
Recorded at Capitol Records, Los Angeles on
August 2, 1960.

6 **Angel Eyes**
(Earl Brent – Matt Dennis)
Ella Fitzgerald: vocals
Barney Kessel: guitar
Recorded in Los Angeles on July 24, 1957.

Black Coffee
(J. Francis Burke – Paul Francis Webster)
Paul Smith: piano
Recorded in Los Angeles on April 14, 1960.

7 **A-Tisket, A-Tasket**
(traditional, arrangement by Ella Fitzgerald –
Van Alexander)

Chick Webb and his band:
Mario Bauza, Taft Jordan,
Boddy Stark: trumpet
George Matthews, Nat Story,
Sandy Williams: trombone
Garvin Bushell: clarinet, alto saxophone
Louis Jordan: alto saxophone, voice
Wayman Carver, Teddy McRae: tenor saxophone
Tommy Fulford: piano
Bobby Johnson: guitar
Beverly Peer: double bass
Chick Webb: drums
Recorded in New York on May 2, 1938.

8 **How High the Moon?**
(Morgan Lewis – Nancy Hamilton)
Small unknown band:
Leonard Graham: trumpet
Ray Brown: double bass
George Russell: arrangement and direction
Recorded in New York on December 20, 1947.

9 **Bewitched, Bothered and Bewildered**
(Richard Charles Rodgers – Lorenz Milton Hart)
Ella Fitzgerald: vocals
Paul Smith: piano
Barney Kessel: guitar
Joe Mondragon: double bass
Alvin Stoller: drums
Recorded Capitol Records Studio B. Hollywood
on August 29, 1956.

10 **Jingle Bells**
(J. S. Pierpont)
Frank DeVol's Orchestra
Ella Fitzgerald: vocals
Recorded at Columbia Recording Studio, New York
on July 15, 1960.

11 **It Don't Mean a Thing (If It Ain't Got That Swing)**
(Duke Ellington)
Ella Fitzgerald: vocals
with the Jimmy Jones Trio: Jimmy Jones: piano;
Jim Hughardt: double bass; Grady Tat: drums
and the Duke Ellington Band: Cat Anderson,
Mercer Ellington, Herbie Jones: trumpet; Lawrence
Brown, Chuck Connors, Buster Cooper: trombone;
Johnny Hodges, Russell Procope: alto saxophone;
Jimmy Hamilton: tenor saxophone , clarinet; Paul
Gonsalves: tenor saxophone
Recorded on July 29 1966, *Ella & Duke at The Côte
d'Azur*, © Verve. With kind permission of the Universal
Music label.

FIRST DISCOVERY MUSIC

JOHANN SEBASTIAN BACH
LUDWIG VAN BEETHOVEN
HECTOR BERLIOZ
FRYDERYK CHOPIN
CLAUDE DEBUSSY
GEORGE FRIDERIC HANDEL
WOLFGANG AMADEUS MOZART
HENRY PURCELL
FRANZ SCHUBERT
PYOTR ILYICH TCHAIKOVSKY
ANTONIO VIVALDI

LOUIS ARMSTRONG
RAY CHARLES
ELLA FITZGERALD